The Rhode Island Colony

Bob Italia

ABDO Publishing Company

visit us at
www.abdopub.com

Published by ABDO Publishing Company, 4940 Viking Drive, Edina, Minnesota 55435.
Copyright © 2001 by Abdo Consulting Group, Inc. International copyrights reserved in all
countries. No part of this book may be reproduced in any form without written permission from
the publisher.

Printed in the United States.

Cover Photo Credit: North Wind Picture Archives
Interior Photo Credits: North Wind Picture Archives (pages 9, 11, 13, 15, 17, 19, 21, 25, 27, 29);
    Corbis (page 7); Library of Congress, Prints and Photographs Division, Historic American
    Buildings Survey, Reproduction Number HABS,RI,4-JONTO,1-3 (page 23)

Contributing Editors: Tamara L. Britton, Kate A. Furlong, and Christine Fournier
Book Design and Graphics: Neil Klinepier

Library of Congress Cataloging-in-Publication Data

Italia, Bob, 1955-
   The Rhode Island Colony / Bob Italia.
     p. cm. -- (The colonies)
   Includes index.
   ISBN 1-57765-587-7
   1. Rhode Island--History--Colonial period, ca. 1600-1775--Juvenile literature. [1.
Rhode Island--History--Colonial period, ca. 1600-1775.] I. Title. II. Series.

F82 .I83 2001
974.5--dc21

            2001022787

Contents

Rhode Island

Native Americans lived in Rhode Island long before the colonists arrived. In 1524, the first European explorer visited Rhode Island. More explorers followed in the early 1600s.

In 1636, English colonists established Rhode Island's first permanent settlement. More colonists soon came to Rhode Island seeking religious freedom. They built their own houses, sewed their own clothes, and grew their own food.

As the colony prospered, so did its **economy**. By the late 1700s, Rhode Island had developed a strong trade with Europe and other colonies.

Then England began passing strict laws and taxes. They hurt Rhode Island's trade. This led to a war. Hundreds of Rhode Islanders fought in it.

In 1776, Rhode Island declared its independence from England. Seven years later, the colonists won the war. They formed the United States of America. Rhode Island became the thirteenth state in 1790.

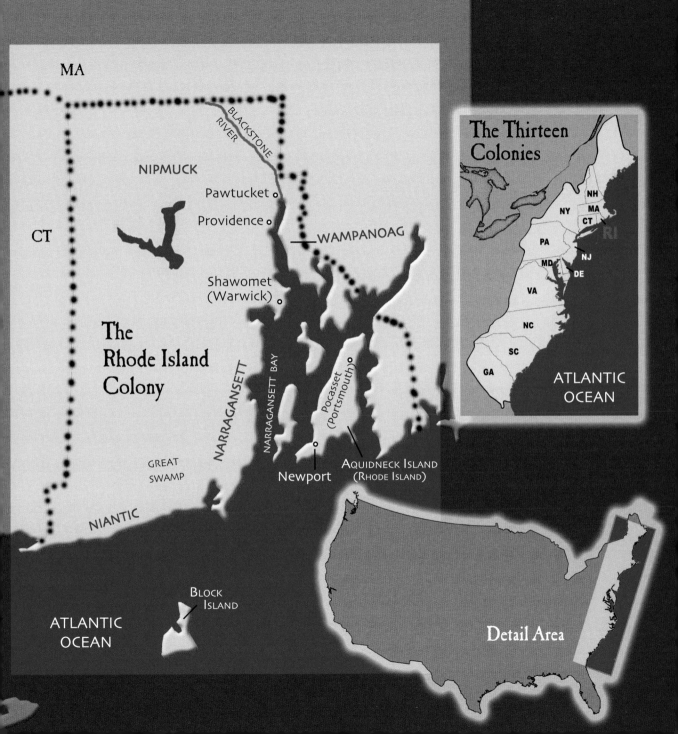

MA

CT

BLACKSTONE
RIVER

NIPMUCK

Pawtucket

Providence

WAMPANOAG

Shawomet
(Warwick)

The
Rhode Island
Colony

NARRAGANSETT

NARRAGANSETT BAY

Pocasset
(Portsmouth)

GREAT
SWAMP

Newport

AQUIDNECK ISLAND
(RHODE ISLAND)

NIANTIC

ATLANTIC
OCEAN

BLOCK
ISLAND

The Thirteen
Colonies

NH
NY   MA
CT
RI
PA
MD   NJ
DE
VA
NC
SC
GA

ATLANTIC
OCEAN

Detail Area

Early History

Rhode Island is located along Narragansett (nare-uh-GAN-suht) Bay. The bay is home to about 35 islands. Hills, rivers, lakes, ponds, and forests cover Rhode Island's land. It has a mild climate.

The area's first settlers were Native Americans. Wampanoags (wahm-puh-NO-agz) lived along the east coast of Narragansett Bay. Narragansetts lived on the bay's west coast. Nipmucks (NIHP-muks) lived inland, just north and west of present-day Providence. Niantics (ni-AN-tiks) lived along the southwest coast.

By 1650, about 10,000 Native Americans lived in Rhode Island. About 6,000 of them were Narragansetts. They were the area's largest Native American group.

Narragansetts spoke the **Algonquian** (al-GON-kwee-an) language. They survived by farming, hunting, and fishing. Leaders called sachems (SAA-chumz) ruled the Narragansetts.

Rhode Island's coastline

The First Explorers

In 1524, Giovanni da Verrazzano (gee-oh-VAH-nee dah ver-rah-ZAH-noh) arrived in present-day Rhode Island. He was the first European to visit the area. He spent two weeks exploring Narragansett Bay. While there, he met Narragansetts and Wampanoags.

Verrazzano also visited present-day Block Island. He compared its size to a Greek island called Rhodes. Verrazzano's comparison provided a name for the future colony.

In 1614, Englishman John Smith explored North America's east coast. He sailed past Rhode Island. Smith made a map of the land along the coast. He named the region New England.

A Dutchman named Adriaen Block also visited the Rhode Island area in 1614. Like Smith, he explored the area and made a good map. One of the islands Block explored was on the southern coast. Later, the island was named after him.

After 1620, colonists from the Plymouth and Massachusetts Bay Colonies traveled to the Rhode Island area. There, they traded with the Native Americans.

Verrazzano's ship sails into Newport's harbor.

9

Settling Rhode Island

William Blackstone moved to Rhode Island in 1635. He was the area's first European settler. He built a farm near present-day Pawtucket. He called his farm Study Hill.

The area's next settler was Roger Williams. He had been living in the Massachusetts Bay Colony. Its government had forced him to leave because of his religious beliefs. So Williams traveled to Rhode Island. He arrived there in 1636.

Williams met with Narragansett sachems. They granted him land at the head of Narragansett Bay. There, Williams founded Providence. It was Rhode Island's first permanent settlement.

In 1638, Anne Hutchinson, John Clarke, and William Coddington founded a settlement on Aquidneck (uh-KWID-nek) Island. They called their settlement Pocasset. Later, it was renamed Portsmouth.

Coddington left Portsmouth after political disagreements. He and his followers moved to southern Aquidneck Island. There, they founded Newport in 1639.

The disagreements in Portsmouth led Samuel Gorton to leave, too. In 1642, Gorton and his followers founded a settlement just south of Providence. They called it Shawomet. It was later renamed Warwick.

Roger Williams builds his house in Providence in 1636.

Government

Rhode Island's four original settlements were Providence, Portsmouth, Newport, and Warwick. At first, they conducted government business in town meetings. They had no judges, courts, or police. When trouble arose, colonists joined together to catch criminals.

After awhile, the settlements faced problems. They had no **charter** for their land. Neighboring colonies wanted to overtake them. So in 1644, Roger Williams secured a charter from England.

The Charter of 1644 said all the settlements were one colony. But some settlements wanted to remain independent. In 1647, all the settlements finally agreed to unite. That year, representatives from each settlement met to form the colony's government.

Rhode Island's government had a ruling body of ten men. A president and four assistants led the group. Rhode Island also had a general assembly. It made the colony's laws. The colony's **freemen** elected members of the government.

In 1663, Rhode Island received a new **charter**. It named the colony Rhode Island and Providence Plantations. It established the colony's land boundaries. It granted colonists religious freedom. And it allowed self-government. The charter served as Rhode Island's basic law until 1843.

Colonists greet Roger Williams as he returns from England with the Charter of 1644.

Life in the Colony

Rhode Island's first towns were located near a source of fresh drinking water. Colonists also built towns near harbors. This made it easier for ships to bring supplies to the colonists.

Goods from England were costly. But early colonists did not have much money. So they had to produce many of the supplies they needed to survive.

Many men farmed. They cleared their fields, raised crops, planted orchards, and kept livestock. They also built their houses and barns. And they ran the government.

Colonial women kept house. They spun thread, wove cloth, sewed clothing, washed laundry, and cleaned the house. They also prepared the meals, preserved foods, and made soap.

Religion was important to Rhode Islanders. Many had been banned from other colonies because of their religious beliefs. But Rhode Island's laws allowed colonists to practice religion freely.

Rhode Island's religious freedom attracted people of many different faiths. In 1639, America's first Baptist church began in Providence. Quakers, Jews, and Huguenots (HEW-ga-notz) also made Rhode Island their home.

Men and women each had important jobs on their farms.

Making a Living

Early colonists bought furs from the Narragansetts. Then they traded the furs for goods from Europe. These goods included Bibles, glass, tools, paper, clothes, spices, and guns.

Soon, colonists began producing their own goods. These included cheese, salt pork, salt fish, and cider. Some colonists built tobacco plantations. They also raised cattle and horses.

Colonists began opening businesses, too. Some colonists worked at sawmills and shipyards. Others operated tanneries that made leather goods. Still others **distilled molasses** to make rum. Rhode Islanders traded these goods with Europe, the West Indies, and other colonies.

Rhode Islanders also bought goods from other countries. The goods came to Rhode Island on large ships. Some of these ships also had slaves aboard.

Slaves worked on some of Rhode Island's plantations. These large farms needed many workers to care for their crops and livestock. But many Rhode Island farms were small. So they did not use slave labor.

The accounting offices of a colonial business

Food

The waters off Rhode Island provided the colonists with plenty of seafood. They caught lobsters, oysters, and clams. They also caught many fish. Colonists preserved their catch by preparing it in salt.

Colonists grew vegetables in their gardens and farms. They grew corn, beans, peas, turnips, parsnips, carrots, and pumpkins. Colonists also gathered berries and nuts in the forests.

Colonial women were responsible for preparing food. They cooked meals in their homes' large fireplace. Women roasted meat on spits. They cooked soup, stew, and vegetables in large pots.

Most homes had a brick oven. It was built into one side of the fireplace. An iron door kept the heat in the oven. Women used these ovens to bake bread, pies, and beans.

Early colonists ate food from plates and cups made of baked clay. Later, colonists began to use dishes made of china and pewter.

The fireplace was at the center of colonial home life. Colonists cooked all of their meals over the open fire.

Clothing

Rich colonists could buy clothes or expensive fabrics from England. But common people could not afford to do this. So women made their own cloth and sewed their own clothing.

Many colonists raised sheep on their farms. Women used spinning wheels to turn the sheeps' wool into thread. Then they used handlooms to weave it into cloth.

Some farmers grew flax. Flax plants have long, silklike fibers inside. Just like wool, flax fibers were spun into thread and woven into fabric. Cloth made from flax fibers is called linen.

Common women wore dresses made of homespun cloth. Rich women wore dresses made of silk, lace, and velvet. Often the dresses had **petticoats** underneath. Women also wore **bonnets** to shield their faces from the sun.

Men and boys wore linen shirts and fitted jackets, called doublets. They wore knee-length pants, called breeches. Men tanned their own leather for shoes and belts.

Rich colonists buy fabric from a store.

Homes

Colonists found plentiful building materials in Rhode Island. They made boards, beams, shingles, and **pitch** from trees. They used clay to make bricks. They built chimneys of stones. They made mortar from **lime**. And they used **rushes** to make thatched roofs.

Some of the colony's early homes were called Rhode Island stone-ender houses. In a stone-ender house, one wall was made of stones. A chimney was built into this stone wall. The lower part of the chimney formed a huge fireplace.

The first stone-ender houses usually had one room. But sometimes families added onto their houses. The most common addition was a shed built off the back wall. Later, colonists built stone-ender houses that were two stories high.

The first colonists had little furniture. They made beds and tables from wood. Chairs were uncommon. Colonists sat on benches and stools instead. They stored family belongings in trunks. Later, colonists made decorative furniture. They also shipped in fine furniture from other countries.

Early colonists used short, thin pieces of pinewood to light their homes. The **pitch** in the wood burned like a torch. Later, colonists made candles out of **tallow**.

A Rhode Island stone-ender house

Children

Colonial children spent most of their time helping their parents with farmwork. There was little time for play. Children were often sick. Many children died when they were babies.

When children had free time, they liked to sing songs and tell stories. They said tongue twisters and told riddles. They also liked to play with hoops, tops, and marbles. In the winter, children ice-skated and sledded.

Boys worked in the fields, shops, and stores. Young men were encouraged to become **apprentices** and learn a trade. Many boys found work at Rhode Island's busy ports. Some boys were only 12 years old when they went to sea.

Girls were expected to learn housekeeping. They learned how to spin thread, sew, cook, and clean.

At first, education was not important to Rhode Island colonists. They did not establish a public school system. Some private schools existed. But most of the children who attended these schools came from wealthy families.

In 1764, colonists founded Rhode Island College. Its name was later changed to Brown University. It is one of America's oldest universities.

A young colonial girl learns how to sew.

Native Americans

Roger Williams kept the Narragansetts and the colonists on friendly terms. The Narragansetts became the colonists' **allies**. In 1637, they helped the colonists attack the Pequot (PEE-kwat) of the Connecticut Colony.

Slowly, the Native Americans grew distrustful of the colonists. Colonists had treated Native Americans poorly. And they had overtaken many Native American lands.

These problems led to King Philip's War in 1675. The war began in the Massachusetts Bay Colony. A Wampanoag chief named Metacom (mee-ta-com) led the Native Americans. The colonists called him King Philip.

The war soon spread to Rhode Island. The Narragansetts tried to remain **neutral**. But the colonists attacked them in Rhode Island's Great Swamp. The attack killed hundreds of Narragansett men, women, and children.

A few months later, the Narragansetts attacked the colonists along the Blackstone River. Eighty-five people died. Then the Narragansetts burned many of Providence's buildings.

After the attack, Metacom died. Many Native Americans lacked food or became ill. The Narragansetts and Wampanoags joined the Niantics, who had remained **neutral**. Slowly, the tribes were pushed from the colony.

Roger Williams tried to build strong relationships with the Native Americans.

The Road to Statehood

Rhode Island prospered in the 1700s. It had established a strong rum trade with the West Indies. In 1764, England passed the Sugar Act. It forced colonists to pay high taxes on **molasses** shipped in from foreign countries. This tax greatly hurt Rhode Island's rum trade.

In the following years, England continued to make new taxes. This angered Rhode Islanders and other colonists.

Rhode Island was among the first colonies to **rebel** against England. The most violent rebellion took place on June 9, 1772. That night, Rhode Islanders attacked and burned an English ship called the *Gaspée*.

In 1775, the **American Revolution** began. No major battles took place in Rhode Island. But hundreds of Rhode Islanders fought in the war. Stephen Hopkins helped form the **Continental** Navy, which his brother Esek led. And Nathanael Greene became one of the Continental Army's great leaders.

On May 4, 1776, Rhode Island declared independence from England. Rhode Island was North America's first free republic.

Colonists officially won the **American Revolution** in 1783. They created the United States of America. Rhode Island became the thirteenth state on May 29, 1790.

Today, Rhode Island is America's smallest state. Jewelry production and tourism make Rhode Island's **economy** strong.

Rhode Islanders burn the *Gaspée*.

TIMELINE

1524 - Giovanni da Verrazzano explores the Rhode Island area

1614 - John Smith and Adriaen Block explore the Rhode Island area

1635 - William Blackstone is first European to settle in the Rhode Island area

1636 - Providence founded

1637 - Narragansetts form alliance with English, fight in war against the Pequot

1638 - Pocasset (Portsmouth) founded

1639 - Newport founded

1642 - Shawomet (Warwick) founded

1644 - Rhode Island receives its first charter

1647 - Providence, Portsmouth, Newport, and Warwick unite as one colony, form government

1663 - Rhode Island receives its second charter

1675 - King Philip's War begins; Great Swamp Fight occurs in Rhode Island

1764 - Sugar Act passes; Brown University founded

1772 - Rhode Island's colonists burn the English ship *Gaspée*

1775 - American Revolution begins

1776 - Rhode Island declares independence from England

1783 - Colonists win American Revolution

1790 - Rhode Island becomes a state

Glossary

Algonquian - a family of Native American languages spoken from Labrador, Canada, to the Carolinas and westward into the Great Plains.

ally - a nation that is linked to another by treaty.

American Revolution - 1775-1783. A war for independence between England and its colonies in North America. The colonists won and created the United States.

apprentice - a person who learns a trade from a skilled worker.

bonnet - a cloth or straw hat tied under the chin and worn by women and children.

charter - a written contract that states a colony's boundaries and form of government.

continental - a word used to describe something of the American colonies.

distill - to heat and cool a liquid in order to make a new liquid, such as alcohol.

economy - the way a colony, state, or nation uses its money, goods, and natural resources.

freemen - men free from bondage or slavery. Freemen often owned land and had the right to vote for assembly members.

lime - a white substance that comes from limestone, shells, or bone.

molasses - the thick, brown syrup produced when sugarcane is processed into sugar.

neutral - not taking sides in a conflict.

petticoat - a skirt worn beneath a dress.

pitch - a dark, sticky substance used for waterproofing and paving.

rebel - to disobey an authority or the government.

rush - a grasslike plant with long, hollow stems.

tallow - the melted fat of cattle and sheep used in making candles and soap.

Web Sites

Rhode Island History
http://www.sec.state.ri.us/submenus/rihstlnk.htm
This site is sponsored by Rhode Island's secretary of state. It has information about Rhode Island's colonial past.

Narragansett Indian Tribe
http://www.narragansett-tribe.org/
The Narragansett Tribal Government sponsors this site. It has information about the tribe's history and culture.

These sites are subject to change. Go to your favorite search engine and type in Rhode Island Colony for more sites.

Index